Shoebox

Donovan Hufnagle

A Publication of The Poetry Box®

Editing & Book Design: Shawn Aveningo Sanders
Cover Design & Photography: Robert R. Sanders

Though some actions, adventures, tears, and chuckles seem real (and some may be), this is partially a work of poetic fiction. Names, dates, and others may have been changed to buffer and blend actuality.

ISBN: 978-1-948461-77-1
Printed in the United States of America.
Wholesale Distribution via Ingram.

Published by The Poetry Box®, 2021
Portland, Oregon
ThePoetryBox.com

Dear Juliana,

You allow a glimpse, a window crack into your dysplasia—not just the physical deterioration of your body but a peek into your emotional corrosion as well.

Your failing hip, crumbling bones, lost heart, torn shoebox, and scars mark the slow struggles you face and still bear on a daily basis. What does the end look like?

You lost dancing. You lost family. You lose to pain every day. But you linger on. You brave it. You succeed in despite of.

This book is only the mist amongst the looming tempest that creeps under the open pane; it starts with your start, your adoption from Russia. But it opens past wounds, cutting new scars where previous scars hide previous pains.

Through the combination of interviews, journals, observations, a shoebox of memories, fact and fiction, and poetic inspiration, a part of you will live on forever in this book—as art—as archive. Thank you, Juliana, for allowing me, us, to lift the window, to sift through your shoebox of memories.

I dedicate this book to you.

Contents

June 9, 1990 7
February 20, 2019 8
June 9, 1990 10
June 10, 1990 11
March 2, 2019 13
March 10, 2019 15
March 30, 2019 17
June 13, 1990 18
April 5, 2019 21
April 12, 2019 22
December 15, 2010 23
April 15, 2019 24
June 15, 2000 25
June 20, 2000 28
June 22, 2000 29
May 3, 2019 31
June 26, 2000 33
July 2, 2000 34

About the Author 37

June 9, 1990

Hope,

Use this journal to tell your new baby sister, Juliana, everything. A gift for you and later a gift for your sister. When she is old enough, give this journal to her. Enjoy Russia and tell me all about it when you return.

Love,
Aunt Bee

February 20, 2019

Dear Hope,

I found a shoebox with letters in it scrounging around in the belly of your closet; it has been untouched for months. Sweaters, blouses, your favorite pair of jeans… you know, the ones with the ripped knees… enshrined but left in the dark. Fitting, I guess. I found the shoebox with letters from you and Mom. And our father. A shoebox about finding me. About bringing me home. About the love that once hovered like clouds and rainbow right after a spring rain. Your curiosity—a girl mousing around before claiming a piece of the gold at the end of that rainbow. Did you really want a sister? Of course, you were more mom than sister to me. Did you want to be a mom? I can't forget you taught me to dance, to twirl on my toes. And my tattoo of hope is for you. Damn, it hurt to mark my ankle, to brand my body, even if it was with hope. For Hope.

We laughed at my pain. It became a family joke—I will soon be in a wheelchair, unable to move my lower half. My bones slowly rotting away into an emptiness. I will be empty. I am empty. Would it have been different if we knew I had dysplasia? Would things have been different with Mom and our father? I know we used to kid, but I think we really do have familial dysplasia. Is my physical and psychological abnormalities because of it—our dysplasia?

Anyway, when I started reading the letters, the shoebox in my belly rumbled. The reflection of the past has made me yearn for a different future. So I write to you to try, to try and keep my hands from cutting, again. My physical scars, my intentional scars for my internal ones, my ones by chance.

I wonder if you can hear me writing, if you can feel the thoughts, the scratch of pencil. I will put this letter in the shoebox with the others. And I will write again.

Your loving sister,
Juli

June 9, 1990

Dear Juliana,

Today is the day before we leave to Russia. I am nine-years-old. I am so excited that I can get you. We waited for eight months to get the papers we needed to finally get you.

I think I'll call you Juli. I'm writing this while on the plane to New York. For the first time! We are just about there and my ears popped. You know when you go into the air really high or fall to the ground your ears pop because of the pressure. We have to take off and land about 4 times before we reach Russia. Do eardrums bruise? Anyway, on the airplane I see the clouds. I wish you could see. I wish you could feel the popcorn in my ears and see the puffy poodle floating by.

Hope

June 10, 1990

Juliana,

I cannot believe we are on our way. We have been working so long and hard towards this. I did not think we would ever get this far. We have had to overcome a lot of obstacles. We are lucky, though. We have had a lot of people praying for us, and the Lord is taking care of things. Your Daddy and I saw you for the first time a couple of weeks ago. You were so scared of us at first. Like rain, salty tears fell from your blues. I wanted you to like us instantly. I fell in love. I can't wait to see you again.

Mommy

• • •

We are at JFK in New York waiting for our plane to leave to London. I can't wait to see and hold you. I will write you later. Love you, my little Russian angel.

Your Father

To the head doctor of the orphanage #

Matveeva V.F.

Declaration

about agreement of adoption (refusal of parental rights)

Name (full):Bogdanova Tatiana Alexandrovna

Date and place of birth(full):October 10, 1979, Moscow

Residence 5th block of Kapotnya #60, Moscow, Russia

Registration: Krasnogo Mayaka 2-427, Moscow, Russia

Passport: 4599786868, issued by OVD Chertanovo Central of Moscow on November 25, 1999

Marital status (married, not married, widowed) : married

Relationship to the child (mother, father, grandmother, grandfather, legal guardian):mother

I request that my child (last name, first name, patronymic in full with the full date of birth): Bogdanova Elena Olegovna, who was born June 5, 1999 in GKB-68(City Hospital) of Moscow, would be transferred on complete state maintenance, because I refuse my parental rights on this child.

The reason for refusal: financial hardship.

I will not oppose to transfer of my child for adoption. I will not have any claims to the adoptive parents. The consequences of the adoption were explained to me.

About myself: height 164 cm, hair color-brown, eye color-greyish-green, nationality-Russian, education(profession)-High school, not on the list in KVD(Dermatology and Venerology clinic), PND(psycho-neurological clinic), ND(drug addiction clinic), PTD(TB clinic).

Information about the father of the child: height 172 cm, hair color-brown, eye color-brown, nationality-Russian, education(profession)-unfinished secondary, not on the list in KVD

March 2, 2019

Dear Hope,

Did you know my name? I mean, I am not sure whether my birth mother named me or if it was the orphanage. Do you remember that movie with Val Kilmar as the thief, *The Saint?* He changed his name to different saints to hide his identity to only find new ones. Is Juli me or am I, Saint? I am definitely not Elena.

I must be only a product—a hollow Matryoshka doll (the same one I came home with)—a product of the orphanage. Why would my birth parents, Tatianna and Oleg, name me if they were only to throw me away? Did you know, in order to be eligible for adoption, Russian children had to have medical conditions. It looks like they wanted to preserve "good" babies as if they were cherished jars of raspberry jam. They wanted to be rid of the spoiled fruit. Did Tatiana know? Was the doll hers? Does she still have the innards, the nesting dolls within?

As I write this, I am falling, sinking into a dark well. I do wish I could have children. I do wish for that one day. A child could be the thing I need, the rope and bucket to pull me from this well. Should I adopt? Another nesting doll? Empty? I wish you could answer me.

Yours,
Nesting Doll

I have paid $14,000.00 for balance on the adoption. $50.00 for registration, $50.00 for documents and $100.00 for airports.

150
x19
2850

14,000
2,850
~~0~~ 100
100
$17,050.00

March 10, 2019

Dear Hope,

OMG! Mom and our father paid a mound of money for me. Was that the extent of our love? Nevertheless, the shoebox is an archive, a safe of memories and facts, though, not reality, at least for me. I found this scrap, this note with numbers on it. Can you believe the cost? I know Mom and our father wanted more babies and they couldn't, but dang! Anyway, I needed to jot this down before I forgot. I'll write soon.

P.S. You never did tell me how much in vitro cost you. Kat is you; I see Hope in her. Your daughter is another shoebox…your shoebox, I guess. All that she does is a memory of you. I wish you could see her.

Juli

Mother and father refused their parental rights on the girl.

Bogdanova Elena Olegovna was evaluated by the government medical committee on January 20, 2000. Diagnoses: perinatal hypoxic encephalopathy in residual period, slow psycho-motor and speech development. Urinary tract infection, open oval window (foramen ovale) without disturbances in hemodynamics.

There was no opportunity to place the girl for adoption with a family of citizens of Russian Federation.

March 30, 2019

Dear Hope,

Pissed! I uncover incomplete adoption papers for another. Did you know Mom and our father didn't even see me at first? Did you? The things I forgot are the very things I want to remember.

I start cutting myself.

I do not have many friends.

I feel like I have nothing—
an empty lightening-bug-mason-jar.

I cut myself on the arm.
I cut myself on my thigh.
I cut here. I cut myself

because I did not care—
a mason jar of dead lightening bugs.

Cutting is escape

like dance use to be.

I hold a mirror up to my scars and they drink in
my skin like watercolor in parchment, but
they hurt so much I never got them colored in.

Do scars understand the chutes and ladders of life?

Your Sis

June 13, 1990

Juli,

Today I visit you at the orphanage. I wait for you to wake. An hour later they bring you—you cry like a fire truck siren. You are really scared of me, I guess. Sooo cute, though! We try to play with you but your siren screams louder and louder. But then you went back to your group and you stop crying.

But Mommy wants to see you again. So she takes you and plays with you. You do not cry this time.

Hope
P.S. Talk to you soon

Dear Juliana,

Today we go to visit you at the orphanage. You cry really hard every time you look at us. I eventually got you to calm down by singing "Bingo." *B I N G O, B I N G O, B I N G O, and Bingo was his name O.* I sing. I also notice a bump on your forehead, a lone hill amongst the desert. I want to get you out of this orphanage so bad. You are so cute today, though. You actually laugh while we play.

Hope is very disappointed that you would not have anything to do with her. I will be glad when you get used to her. She is going to be a great big sister.

Mommy

J—

Today we take your big sister, Hope, to see you. Your hair is all messed up from taking a nap. A spiked and Pollack splatter.

We can not get you calmed down. Just when it seems you are about to settle, you take one glance at me and you start to cry again. Will I ever be your father? Whenever you look my way you start to cry again.

You Father

April 5, 2019

Dear Hope,

My scars are not my feelings, fantasies or fairytales,
but my scars feel and remember; they dredge what
has been seen without being said—a silent narrative.

I had to change my whole lifestyle.
My first surgery was scheduled for November.
There are times I wish there were troubleshooting
instructions, a reboot option.

I was 15 years old and my world shattered
like ceramic doll legs in a infant's hands.
And this began my long medical
journey I still deal with
today.

Juli

April 12, 2019

Dear Hope,

I enter death every time I flirt
with my skin, like a hollow rendezvous
with my mister; he is my seducer of pain.
Or am I the seducer? I cut myself to see
if I'm still alive. I cut myself to see
if I will die.

How do you put a name to your feelings? How
do you take something intangible and make it
actual? How? I cut myself to see if I will
die. I cut myself to see if I'm still
alive.

The blood weeps from my body as if my skin
is an overwrought rag, exhausted from being
from being, the barrier between life
and the other, between in and out. I cut
to see if I am still alive, if I will die.

I'm mesmerized by how
the red scars the water, by how
the pain, now, doesn't just exist within the opaque,
the marrow but resides in the transparent,
without. I cut myself to see if I will die, to see
if I am alive.

I cut myself to see.

Juli

December 15, 2010

Body,

I never knew I would go through this much
at my age. I feel like I am constant, always divided,
two lands at war, the mind mutilating you and
you—scarring the mind. You are so beautiful, yet a
poison, my little Angel's Trumpet. Some days I can't
even move out of bed and some days I don't
want to. The scars you have left … I am humiliated
and cut. Like lifeless rivers and streams, the scars
cross my hips, thighs, and my memories. They
remember. Timelessness. I have scars.
Some days hurt too much. Other days
just hurt.

I am tired of being this pain.

Regretfully Yours

April 15, 2019

Dear Hope,

It is difficult to write today. Mom hands me the rest of the matryoska doll, the doll within the doll, within the doll, within the doll, within the doll. She tells me that you gave me the doll and held the inside dolls until I had a baby of my own. If only. The emptiness is nesting. Thank you. I miss you.

Juli

June 15, 2000

Dear Juliana,

Today we have our court hearing. You are ours, finally. But we have to wait ten days before the courts release you to us. Ten days of agony. Time holds his two wands over our head, and He doesn't race to the finish line quickly.

We visit you later today. We play. Peak A Boo! Where are you? Before you cry. Today, with my hands springing out like French doors, revealing my once covered face, you smile. You even smile and laugh at your father, some.

Mommy

Buy power concentrators

~~Call Dr. Morrow~~

Call Dr. Bullard

Order Colloidal Silver

~~Add Kristen to ins.~~

Order bird house

~~Travel arrangements~~

Set up Pat Riddle

Set up summer stuff (CATS)

~~Pay tuition~~

~~Buy hot plate~~

Order fathers day gift

Order shots - K

Order checks

J—

As usual your hair is a mess when we pick you up—a twister of neglect. A whirling bird's nest. You cry at first. You cry again when you look at me. But you play on the faux hardwood floor with Mommy and Hope. The floor is a triangle pattern, like arrows pointing toward the door. Without the hinge of green creeping on most of the floor, it could be confused for real wood.

Your Father

June 20, 2000

Juli,

This lady told us to sit in the music room. I thought, "cool," music, but the room only had a wounded piano with its flesh tearing from its bones, some of its teeth broken or missing. Its legs look like they were quivering from the pain of standing too long.

Ten minutes later, the lady brings you to me. She hands you over like a fragile nesting doll. I bought you one today. A doll. I took the innards out, so you wouldn't choke. I'll put them in a piece at a time as we grow up together. You are smiling. You didn't cry. You didn't cry!

Oops! I forgot to tell you. We pray to God that we can take you home.

P.S. I have some pictures I took. I will show you later.

I love you,
Hope

June 22, 2000

Juliana,

Well, we are having a nice visit with you today. Unfortunately, as if my plastic spoon snapped in two in the pudding, we find out that we can't bring you home until Monday. I am sad. They string us along and along, day after day. It is so hard to let you go, back to your group.

Forever Yours,
Mommy

>>Hello Carreen. Allison told me you would be writing. I actually used to
>>work at the American Embassy and I handled adoptions. It was a long time
>>ago - 1992-1993, so I know a lot has changed probably for the better. Do
>>you know what town you will be traveling to? What organization are you
>>working with?
>>
>>As far as sights to see and places to go - there is a lot to see here in
>>Moscow. Great musuems, the Kremlin, theatre, etc. You may be surprised
to
>>see that Moscow is a busy, big, cosmopolitan city. There is lots of
>>traffic and there are lots of people. I would suggest getting a guide to
>>take you out to Zagorsk which is about an hour outside the city. It is an
>>old town filled with churches. I have not been there in a long time. I
>>think it has probably gotten more touristy but I think it is worth taking
a
>>trip outside the city. There is a tour company that can arrange just
>>about any tour you would like with a guide and driver if needed. It is
>>called Patriarch's Dom and the number is 795 0927.
>>
>>There are lots of great restaurants here now. A lot are very expensive
and
>>some are not so. For dinner it is a good idea to get reservations. Here
>>is a list of ones I like:
>>
>>Il Pomodoro - great homey Italian, run by Italians, my favorite,
reasonably
>>priced - 924-2931 Bolshoi Golovin Pereulok #2/5.
>>Starlite Diner - American diner owned by Americans, hamburgers, shakes,
>>great if you are missing home a bit - no reservations. There is one at
>>Mayakovsky Square and another at Oktyabrskaya Square.
>>Uncle Guilley's - same owners as above - great steak a little pricey but
>>good food - 229-2050 Stoleshnikov Pereulok #6.
>>Bochka - Russian food - great meat - rustic atmosphere - my husband's
>>favorite restaurant - a little pricey - 252 -3041 - 1905 Goda #2.
>>Guria - Great Georgian food! - cheap and fabulous, get the Khachapuri
>>(cheese bread) - Kommsomolsky Prosp. 7/3. Do not miss this one! It is a
>>little grungy inside and the wait staff is not very friendly but they have
>>the menus in English so you won't need any help ordering.
>>
>>As far as things to bring for gifts I am a little bit at a loss because
you
>>can literally get everything here now. It used to be that people brought
>>stockings and make up for women but believe me there is no shortage on
>>these anymore. I would suggest something distinctly Texas (I assume you
>>are from Texas, right?) If not, then from your state. When I am bringing
>>things back for my mother-in-law or our nanny I usually go to the Gap and
>>find something there. I wish I could be more helpful with this one but
you
>>will see when you get here that really there are no shortages here, so you
>>do not need to worry about trying to bring something that you can't find

May 3, 2019

Hope,

It has been a bit, a sliver in time since I have written. I have read all the wonderful letters written to me, and as you can see, I have added a bit more, but this may be my last. Unfortunately, I still feel broken. I feel abandoned like I was so long ago by Tatiana, wasting on the doorsteps of the orphanage until you found me.

Again, I am wasting away, forgotten on another doorstep, so to speak. The very house I grew up in, learned to ride my Huffy—thank you, by the way—learned to twirl and tiptoe, tap and tombé, played dress up and hide and seek. This time I am abandoned by my body. Our father. And Mom. And you.

As you know, my hip didn't start aching, scratching with its talons until I was about thirteen-years-old. I guess the more I danced, the more I developed, the more I was disappearing—one Matryoshka doll after another—the body, the mind, the heart, the spirit, and, finally, the soul. My soul sank away as the layers of my bones faded.

Most of the time, dancers ignore pain like loose hairs floating away with the wind. Ignoring that we are born to die. I brushed the pain away as did the doctors.

I don't think the doctors believed in my pain, my dysplasia. Nor the physical therapists, the chiropractors, the psychologists, the many specialist, and, of course, God.

After my surgeries, he told me that my lifetime of pain will continue…that the giant that symbolizes my former days has now become the mouse trapped without hope of escape. Dance was my entire life, and I will never dance again.

This time when I need family the most, I have dysplasia. I have nothing, except Kat. I have been abandoned by our father. But let's face it, he was really never there. And since our father left, Mom has dissolved to A and B actions, the simplest of tasks take so much effort for her. I barely can walk let alone float across a dance stage. I can't even dance in front of the mirror in the bathroom. My surgeries have removed any chance of children. I am afraid to adopt.

And You. Why did you die?

I miss you.

Yours,
Juliana

June 26, 2000

Juli,

We finally get to bring you home today. I am so excited. You greet me with a smile. You wear the new clothes we bought for you. You are holding the doll I gave you. I hope you keep it forever. We take you back to our hotel. We give you a bath. You don't like baths. You nap for two hours. You wake and eat dinner: chicken noodle soup, sweet potatoes, banana, and cheese. You go to bed. We are looking forward to starting our life with you.

Love Always,
Mommy

P.S. Hope cried happy thoughts when we took you from the orphanage. She held you the whole way to the apartment. She will be your rock.

July 2, 2000

Juliana,

You are so precious! What a beautiful smile. Our family is so blessed. "It will be so easy to love you. You are so precious," I thought. I am so excited to watch you grow up with our family.

We all love you so dearly.

God bless,
Aunt Bee

About the Author

Donovan Hufnagle learned late in life that his great, great aunt was proposed to by Conrad Hilton. Unfortunately, she declined because she didn't want children. So instead of making questionable videos as if he were Paris Hilton, Donovan Hufnagle writes; it's better that way.

Donovan is a father of three, a husband, and a professor of English and Humanities. He moved from Southern California to Prescott, Arizona to Fort Worth, Texas. His book, *The Sunshine Special,* published in 2018, is "part personal narrative, epic poem, and historical artifact." Other recent writings have appeared in *Beyond Words, Wingless Dreamer, Subprimal Poetry Art, Americana Popular Culture Magazine, Shufpoetry, Kitty Litter Press, Carbon Culture, Amarillo Bay, Borderlands, Tattoo Highway, The New York Quarterly, Rougarou,* and others.

<donovanhufnagle.com>

About The Poetry Box®

The Poetry Box® is a boutique publishing company in Portland, Oregon, who provides a platform for both established and emerging poets to share their words with the world through beautiful printed books and chapbooks.

Feel free to visit the online bookstore (thePoetryBox.com), where you'll find more titles including:

Nothing More to Lose by Carolyn Martin

Many Sparrows by donnarkevic

Like the O in Hope by Jeanne Julian

A Shape of Sky by Cathy Cain

The Very Rich Hours by Gregory Loselle

Shadow Man by Margaret Chula

Between States of Matter by Sherry Rind

The Kingdom of Birds by Joan Colby

Off Coldwater Canyon by C.W. Emerson

Excoriation by Rebecca Smolen

Mouth Quill by Kaja Weeks

and more . . .

www.ingramcontent.com/pod-product-compliance
Ingram Content Group UK Ltd.
Pitfield, Milton Keynes, MK11 3LW, UK
UKHW020136250726
13967UKWH00002B/698